Bessie Smith

Alexandria Manera

Raintree

Chicago, Illinois

VISUAL & PERFORMING ARTS

For information, address the publisher
Raintree, 100 N. LaSalle, Suite 1200, Chicago, IL 60602

Printed and bound in the United States by Lake Book Manufacturing, Inc.
07 06 05 04 03
10 9 8 7 6 5 4 3 2 1

Library of Congress Cataloging-in-Publication Data

Manera, Alexandria.
  Bessie Smith / Alexandria Manera.
      p. cm. -- (African American biographies)
Summary: Recounts the life of the famous blues singer who flourished during the 1920s.
Includes bibliographical references (p.   ) and index.
  ISBN 0-7398-6875-6 (HC), 1-4109-0034-7 (Pbk.)
  1. Smith, Bessie, 1898?-1937--Juvenile literature. 2. Singers--United States--Biography--Juvenile literature. 3. Blues (Music)--History and criticism--Juvenile literature. [1. Smith, Bessie, 1898?-1937. 2. Singers. 3. Women--Biography. 4. African Americans--Biography. 5. Blues (Music)] I. Title. II. Series: African American biographies (Chicago, Ill.)
  ML3930.S67 M36 2003
  782.421643'092--dc21

                    2002153361c

Acknowledgments
The publishers would like to thank the following for permission to reproduce photographs:
pp. 4, 10, 15, 26, 57, 58 Bettmann/CORBIS; p. 6 CORBIS; pp. 8, 16, 22, 30, 36, 47, 52 Hulton/Archive by Getty Images; pp. 12, 20, 25, 28, 48, 51 Underwood & Underwood/CORBIS; pp. 18, 34 Associated Press, AP; pp. 39, 55 Library of Congress.

Cover photograph: Bettmann/CORBIS

Content Consultant
Kai Fikentscher
School of Contemporary Arts
Ramapo College of New Jersey

Some words are shown in bold, **like this.** You can find out what they mean by looking in the Glossary.

Contents

Young Bessie Smith was the highest-paid African-American performer of her time. Pictures of her such as this one were used on her records and in advertisements for her shows.

Introduction

Some people believe that Bessie Smith is the greatest blues singer of all time. Her strong voice and popular songs have made her one of the most famous African Americans in history.

After many years of struggling and a lot of hard work, Bessie Smith became a huge success. Smith began her career in 1912 and sang the blues until she died in 1937. During this time, she recorded nearly 160 songs. Her music became so popular that people called her the "Empress of the Blues." Even today, musicians still study her work.

Understanding the Blues

The blues is a type of music. It began in the southern United States after the Civil War (1861–1865). The Civil War was a war between the Northern states and Southern states. Northern states wanted to end slavery, and Southern states wanted to keep slaves. This issue started the war.

Blues music was born out of the lyrics and oral tradition of slaves' hardships. After slavery, men carried on the blues tradition, singing about hard times and the unfair treatment of African Americans.

No one is sure exactly where or how blues music started. Most people believe the blues began in the farming areas of the South. There, African-American slaves worked long, hard days on large farms called plantations. The slaves called to each other while they worked in the field. Over time, these calls and sounds became songs. The long, often sad songs had a special musical style.

Many of the **lyrics** (song words) came from African-American **oral tradition,** which are stories that have been passed down from one generation to the next by word of mouth. The songs were often about slavery and the unfair treatment of African Americans. Many continued to sing the blues long after slavery was outlawed.

After slavery, men carried on the blues tradition. They sang the blues while they played the guitar. They played in bars and other small shows to a mostly African-American audience. It was not until the early 1900s that women began singing the blues, too.

Through the years, blues has become even more popular. Today, most blues lyrics follow an easy three-line pattern. Words in these lines often repeat, and the tune is usually simple. The following is an example of a three-line blues pattern:

> *Mississippi River, what a fix you left me in*
> *Mississippi River, what a fix you left me in*
> *Mudholes of water clear up to my chin.*

Bessie discovered her talent for singing at an early age when she sang for money after her parents died.

Chapter 1:
Smith's Early Days

Not much is known about Bessie Smith's childhood. People only began to write about her when she was a famous singer. Even then, most of the stories were about her songs, not her life.

Blues singers such as Smith often sang about people they loved and the problems in their lives. Bessie Smith had a hard life full of a lot of sadness to sing about. Some people say that she actually lived the blues.

For Smith, trouble began at an early age. She was born in Chattanooga, Tennessee. Her exact date of birth is not known. Many people think she was born on April 15, 1894, but her gravestone says she was born in 1895. During the late 1800s, many African-American births were not written down on paper. African Americans often used **oral tradition** to remember their births.

This is an early electric railroad car in Chattanooga, Tennessee. The picture was taken around 1900 when Bessie was growing up.

By the time Bessie Smith was born, Chattanooga was an important trading city. About 30,000 people lived there. Nearly half of these people were African American.

As in many growing cities, there were many poor people. There were not enough homes or jobs for the many people moving to the city. Too many people crowded together in small homes and apartments. The overcrowding caused unclean conditions that often made people sick.

Life was hard for many African Americans who lived in the early 1900s. Although slavery had ended in 1865, many people still treated African Americans unfairly because of the color of their skin. The United States was **segregated.** This system separated African Americans and whites. Whites lived with other whites. African Americans lived with other African Americans. At that time, many businesses hired whites instead of African Americans.

With so few jobs in the city, it was hard for African Americans to make enough money to live. Bessie Smith was born into a poor African-American family. Her father William was a part-time Baptist preacher. He also ran a mission in downtown Chattanooga. Her mother, Laura Smith, gave birth to eight children. Bessie was the youngest. One died before Bessie was born. Shortly after Bessie was born, her father died, too. By the time she was nine years old, her mother and another brother had also died.

Segregation and lack of job opportunities made life hard for Bessie and other African-American families like this one.

Without a mother or father, the six remaining children had to take care of themselves. The oldest sister Viola took charge of the remaining family—Bessie, Tinnie, Lulu, Clarence, and Andrew. But Viola did not make enough money to feed all her brothers and sisters. So at nine years old, Bessie and the other children began looking for work, too.

Working for Pennies

Bessie and her brother Andrew spent their days working on the streets of downtown Chattanooga. Andrew played the guitar well, and Bessie sang. Sometimes people passing by gave them money. They were lucky if they brought home pennies, nickels, and dimes after a long day of work.

During this time, Bessie Smith discovered her natural talent for music. Her voice was loud and clear for such a small child. She did not know that her talent would change the world of music. Soon her pennies would turn into a fortune.

The Moses Stokes Show

Bessie was not the only talented member of her family. Her older brother, Clarence, was a dancer. The Moses Stokes Traveling Show was a popular **minstrel show.** Minstrel shows were traveling road shows. The shows were about African-American characters, and the performers wore black makeup on their faces. Each show included several acts and ended with a skit. Singers, dancers, actors, comedians, acrobats, and even jugglers performed on stage. Clarence was hired by the Moses Stokes Traveling Show to perform as a dancer and comedian. For a while, Clarence traveled with the show. In 1912, he returned to Chattanooga. While in Chattanooga, he arranged for Bessie to **audition,** or try out, for a part in the show.

Bessie was hired by the Moses Stokes Traveling Show when she was just 18 years old. This was her first real job in show business, although it was not as a singer. Bessie, like Clarence, was hired as a dancer in the company. Bessie performed with the Moses

Minstrel Shows

Minstrel shows were about the lives of African Americans, so white actors wore black makeup on their faces. Some of the shows were about African Americans missing their lives as slaves. These shows did not truly represent the lives and feelings of African-Americans. They contained many stereotypes. A stereotype is an overly simple, often incorrect, picture or opinion of a group of people.

Over time, African Americans with musical or acting talent got the chance to join minstrel shows, too. Many had to wear black makeup because they were not thought to be dark enough. However, minstrel shows offered one of the few chances for African Americans to earn a lot of money and travel. Many white businessmen owned these traveling shows. This was one of the first times that whites and African Americans worked together.

African-American performers and musicians found work in traveling minstrel shows like this one in the early 1900s.

Gertrude "Ma" Rainey was the first classic blues singer. She became known as the "Mother of the Blues."

Stokes show for only a short time before moving on to another show. Yet those few months proved important to her singing career.

Meeting "Ma" Rainey

Bessie Smith met Gertrude "Ma" Rainey while performing with the Moses Stokes Traveling Show. Rainey is considered the first woman to sing the blues. Before her, only men sang the blues in shows. Like Smith, Ma Rainey also began her singing career at a young age. In 1900, at the age of 14, Rainey went to work for the Springer Opera House in Columbus, Georgia. For more than 35 years, Ma Rainey toured the country and sang the **classic blues.**

Before Ma Rainey, the classic blues did not exist. The classic blues was a style of music that grew out of **country blues.** The difference was that women sang the classic blues. Men sang the country blues. Famous country blues singers include Blind Lemon Jefferson and Mississippi John Hurt.

Many people call Ma Rainey the "Mother of the Blues" because she was the first classic blues singer. Ma Rainey was the most successful blues singer at the time. But that changed as soon as Bessie Smith began performing music.

Many rumors spread when Ma Rainey and Bessie Smith started singing together. One story claimed that Ma Rainey kidnapped Bessie Smith and forced her to work for her show, *The Rabbit Foot Minstrels.* Other rumors claimed that Rainey taught Smith how to sing the blues. Neither of these stories was true. Smith had been singing the blues long before meeting Ma Rainey.

Ma Rainey was just a close friend to Bessie Smith. Smith looked up to Rainey, who was quite a bit older. Rainey's voice and

Ma Rainey talks with a young man on stage during her show, The Rabbit Foot Minstrels.

talent on stage inspired Smith. Soon Smith's own talent would lead her to become even more successful than Rainey.

Hard at Work

Irvin C. Miller was a well-known owner of two **minstrel shows.** Both of his minstrel shows were touring in 1912. Many owners hired women for both their talent and their appearance. If they did not have good looks, their talent did not matter. Smith was hired to sing in the chorus for one of Miller's shows, but Miller did not approve of Smith's looks.

Bessie Smith was a large-framed woman. She was nearly six feet tall and weighed almost 200 pounds. She was a very dark-skinned African-American woman. In those days, African Americans with darker skin were **discriminated** against more than other African Americans. Some felt that a darker complexion was not as beautiful as a lighter one.

Discrimination did not stop Bessie Smith. She was hard at work and determined to become a success.

In 1913, she moved to Georgia after touring with the Moses Stokes show and Irvin Miller. Once there, she quickly became a regular performer at the "81" Theater in Atlanta, Georgia. Charles Bailey, the theater's owner, hired her to train the chorus girls. At the time, she was making less than ten dollars a week, but her popularity was growing by the day.

It is unclear exactly how long Smith worked for Charles Bailey and the "81" Theater. She took breaks from the theater to tour the South. Her singing gathered new fans wherever she went. After her tours, she returned to the "81" Theater.

Bessie Smith performed in vaudeville theaters around the country, like this one on Broadway in New York City.

Bessie Smith was becoming well known by touring regularly on the **vaudeville** circuit. The vaudeville circuit was a group of theaters that also encouraged African Americans. Like **minstrel shows,** vaudeville shows were variety shows, made up of different singing, dancing, juggling, and acting pieces. But vaudeville shows were not mainly about African Americans and performers did not wear black makeup. The shows were usually performed in one theater and often did not travel around as minstrel shows did.

Vaudeville shows had between eight and fourteen different acts. Vaudeville shows included many talented African-American singers, dancers, magicians, acrobats, jugglers, and comedians.

Smith performed with several companies on the vaudeville circuit. She played for one show called *The Florida Blossoms*. She even had her own show called *The Liberty Blossoms*. All types of people were beginning to notice the African-American performers. At times, they were even asked to perform with white entertainers. Still, the African Americans were forced to stay in separate hotels. They even had to eat at separate restaurants. African-American music was surely making progress, but there was little progress being made to end the **segregation.**

Smith continued to tour the South and parts of the North. Smith had fans packing the theaters to hear her perform. It did not matter where she went because there always seemed to be a crowd. Her career was certainly on the rise. The first advertisement for a Smith show appeared on September 13, 1918, in a Maryland newspaper. She was now a well-known singer. Soon she would be famous.

Mamie Smith recorded "Crazy Blues," in 1920, which was the first blues song recorded by a female African American.

Chapter 2:
The Rise of Her Career

In the early 1920s, Bessie Smith married a man named Earl Love. Unfortunately for Smith, he died shortly after they were married.

While Smith was busy touring the northern theaters, other blues singers were recording songs. In 1920, Mamie Smith (no relation to Bessie) was the first African-American woman to record a blues song. The song was called "Crazy Blues." The record sold hundreds of copies during the first month of its release and changed the record industry forever.

Around 1921, Smith decided to move north to Philadelphia, Pennsylvania. She was active in many shows. By this time, she was often the **headliner,** or main act. She even performed with her own band. She was also a regular singer at the Standard and Dunbar Theaters in Philadelphia.

By the summer of 1922, Smith went to work at the Paradise Gardens, a resort in Atlantic City, New Jersey. It was popular with wealthy people. Smith was beginning to entertain a new kind of crowd—wealthy and white.

Bessie Smith had an amazing power. Her music appealed to people of all backgrounds. It did not matter if they were rich or poor, black or white. Everyone was drawn to her voice and the **lyrics** of her songs.

Falling in Love

Bessie Smith sang from the heart. Her songs often spoke about life, love, and the hard times she lived. Love was a subject Bessie Smith knew well.

Bessie Smith fell in love with a man named Jack Gee. Gee had seen Smith when she was performing in Atlantic City. Later in 1922, Bessie Smith met Jack Gee at a theater in Philadelphia.

On the evening of their first date, Gee was involved in a shooting. He was badly wounded by the gunshot. The event nearly took his life.

While Gee was in the hospital, he and Smith became close friends. She visited him nearly every day for the five weeks he was

Bessie Smith sometimes sang at the exclusive Cotton Club. This was one of the most popular nightclubs in Harlem during the Harlem Renaissance.

in the hospital. Smith and Gee fell madly in love. They moved in together shortly after he was released.

Little Success with the Record Industry

The record industry was booming in New York City. Many people were interested in making records. It seemed as if everyone wanted to be a part of the growing industry.

Bessie Smith made her first record with Columbia Records in 1923.

Bessie Smith auditioned for several record companies. In January 1923, she **auditioned** for Okeh. Okeh was the company that produced the first blues record. Unfortunately, the Okeh record company turned her down. Smith had a very distinct (clearly different) sound. Her voice was so powerful that many record companies thought it was too rough. The companies were looking for a smoother sound more like the white pop singers of the time. This made it difficult for Smith to get a job in the record industry.

After being turned down by Okeh records, Smith decided to sing in the musical show *How Come?* The show played at the Dunbar Theater in Philadelphia. Smith was fired within one week after having a fight with the show's director.

The Discovery

The record industry took credit for discovering Bessie Smith in 1923. However, by this time Smith had become famous on her own. She had fans throughout the country by the time she recorded her first record.

Bessie Smith's recording **debut**, or first record, was with Columbia records. Smith met with Frank Walker, the man in charge of Columbia's recordings.

Walker had heard Bessie Smith sing back in 1917. He knew that Smith had a lot of talent.

The Big Debut

In February of 1923, Frank Walker sent for Bessie Smith. At the time, she was living in Philadelphia with Jack Gee. Smith and Gee traveled to New York to make her first record.

In New York, they stayed with Gee's mother who lived in Harlem, a neighborhood in New York City. It was popular for many African Americans to live in Harlem at this time. During a period

Young Langston Hughes (seen here in a busboy uniform) waited on tables to support himself until his writing became successful.

of time called the **Harlem Renaissance,** this part of town became a center for many talented African-American writers, artists, and musicians. Harlem was an important part of New York City with its own musical style.

The music in Harlem was much different from the music in the South. In the evenings, Smith visited Harlem's theaters and nightclubs. She spent her days preparing for her big debut.

Langston Hughes and the Harlem Renaissance

The **Harlem Renaissance** is an important part of history. In the late 1920s and 1930s, many African Americans made their way to Harlem, a neighborhood in New York City. Thousands of African Americans had settled in the northern states because of new job opportunities. Harlem became the cultural center for a community of African-American thinkers, writers, artists, and musicians.

During this time, many African Americans were educated. People united to make life better for African Americans. They wanted to end **discrimination** and unequal treatment. Many important African Americans, such as Langston Hughes, came out of Harlem during this time.

Langston Hughes (1902–1967) is well known for his poetry. For more than 40 years, Hughes wrote about life as an African American. In 1926, Hughes published his first collection of poems called, *The Weary Blues.* He was influenced by the rhythm of blues and **jazz** music.

Like Bessie Smith, Langston Hughes's work talked about hard times for African Americans. He thought it was fair to talk about life for all African Americans, not just those who were in Harlem. Some of his most important work helped African Americans in their struggle for equal treatment.

This musician plays her cello into a large horn sticking out of the wall. A device on the other side of the wall records her music. This is how all music was recorded in the early 1920s.

Jack Gee had very little money before meeting Bessie Smith. He had a low-paying job as a night guard. Even so, he wanted Smith to have something nice for her first day in the recording studio. He decided to sell his watch and work uniform so he could buy her a new dress. She was very impressed by his kindness.

On February 15, 1923, Bessie Smith went into the Columbia recording studio. Frank Walker thought Smith looked very nervous.

Recording music during the early 1920s was done without using a microphone. The performer sang into a large horn from behind a curtained wall. A person sat on the other side of the wall with a recording device. At the time, there was no way to correct a mistake that was made. The performer would sing the song several times before getting it right.

Bessie Smith tried recording two songs that day. The first song was called "T'ain't Nobody's Business if I Do." Smith tried more than nine times, but was unable to get it right. Then she tried to sing another song called "Down Hearted Blues." She tried that song twice, but could not get it right. Neither song was recorded that day. Smith may have been nervous after all.

Smith went back into the recording studio the very next day. This time, she had more success. Bessie Smith recorded her first song, "Down Hearted Blues," after three tries. Later that day she went on to record another song called the "Gulf Coast Blues."

A Recording Contract

Bessie Smith was working hard for low pay before her recording contract with Columbia. She was making just $125 dollars per song. However, she was cheated out of most of the money because she did not have a good contract.

On April 20, 1923, Frank Walker offered Bessie Smith a one-year recording contract with Columbia. The new contract promised her $1,500 up front and $150 for each record that she made. This was an offer that Smith could not refuse. In time, this contract would bring her great fame and fortune.

Lyrics Written by Bessie Smith

Bessie Smith wrote songs about hard times and sadness around her.
Her music was popular, and people could understand the **lyrics** well.
During the **Great Depression,** thousands of people lost their jobs.
Many people, especially African Americans, were poor and homeless.
Bessie Smith wrote this song about the life of a poor man:

> Mister rich man, rich man, open up
> > your heart and mind,
> Mister rich man, rich man, open up
> > your heart and mind;
> Give the poor man a chance, help
> > stop these hard, hard times.
>
> While you're living in your mansion, you
> > don't know what hard times mean,
> While you're living in your mansion, you
> > don't know what hard times mean,
> Poor working man's wife is starving; your
> > wife is living like a queen.

Bessie Smith smiles as she walks onto the stage to begin a performance.

Chapter 3:
At the Top

Bessie Smith's first record, "Down Hearted Blues," was released in June of 1923. It sold more than 780,000 copies in the first six months. She released five other records around this time, too. All were a success. People were buying her records, listening to her music, and eager to see her in person.

Bessie Smith's hard work was beginning to pay off. Her career was on the rise. Smith finally had a record company that paid her well and advertised her work. She was also preparing for another tour.

Before leaving for her tour, Bessie Smith decided to marry Jack Gee. On June 7, 1923, they went to the Orphan's Court of Philadelphia County to get married.

When she performed on stage, young Bessie Smith wore specially designed fancy gowns and elaborate hats like these.

Bessie spent nearly the entire summer on the road doing shows without her husband. Gee was unable to travel because he was still working as a night guard. Their time apart did not last long. Gee soon quit his job to spend more time with Smith. The money was pouring in from Smith's contract, so it was not necessary for him to work.

Headlining

Bessie Smith was the **headliner** at many theaters. People came from all around to see Smith perform. Many times, there would be lines of people waiting to see her sold-out show.

When Bessie Smith sang, nothing else mattered. While other performers would sing and dance, Bessie preferred just to sing. She was not much of a dancer. When she danced, her movements were rather simple back-and-forth movements. Her powerful voice was enough to fascinate the audience and keep them interested.

People have said that Smith looked graceful performing on stage. She wore many beautiful costumes. Her dresses were often made of satin and sometimes had hanging trim. She was also known to wear wild caps with feathers, beads, or pearls to match her clothing. Her confidence and presence on stage made her an outstanding performer.

Bessie Smith continued singing the blues in cities with large numbers of African Americans. She visited St. Louis, Detroit, Kansas City, and Chicago. Bessie Smith was also getting paid a lot of money for making special guest appearances.

Firsts

There were no African-American women as famous as Bessie Smith during this time. She was one of the first women to be played on the radio. Her music was broadcast over an Atlanta radio station that was mainly for white Southerners. But it did not matter that Smith was African American. They respected her talent.

Bessie Smith was also one of the only African Americans to perform for an "all-white" audience. This never pleased her. She preferred to sing for those who understood the hardships of being an African American in a **segregated** country.

Bessie Smith became the highest paid African-American entertainer. She was making as much as $2,000 per week.

Generous Bessie

For most African Americans, life was difficult during this time. Yet, Smith had remarkable success. She was aware of her good luck and thought often about the poor life she had once lived. She remembered living in poor conditions and working hard just to make a few pennies.

Bessie Smith was a generous woman and was always concerned about her friends and family. Smith often gave money to help her family and many of her friends. In 1926, Smith even adopted a boy from a friend in trouble. Smith named him Jack Junior, after her husband, Jack Gee.

The sadness from Smith's own life helped her sing and write music that helped other people cope with the sadness in their lives.

Eight Strong Years

Bessie Smith remained a top star for eight years. From 1923 until 1931, Smith's popularity was unmatched.

In 1924 and 1925, Smith went back to New York for several more recordings. During this time, Smith recorded the best songs of her career. She was now working with the most talented performers in the music industry, like cornet player Louis Armstrong. Armstrong is perhaps the best-known male musician from this period of time.

Louis Armstrong and Jazz Music

Louis Armstrong is one of the most respected **jazz** musicians of all time. His unique style has influenced musicians of all kinds.

Louis Armstrong

Louis Armstrong was born on August 4, 1901, in New Orleans, Louisiana. Much like Bessie Smith, Armstrong was born into a poor African-American family.

He also showed his musical talent at an early age. In 1915, Armstrong got his first cornet and taught himself how to play.

Armstrong's hard work and practice paid off. In 1922, Armstrong went to Chicago to play in Joe "King" Oliver's jazz band. This was a leading jazz band at the time. In 1925, Armstrong made recordings with a band of his own called the "Hot Five."

Louis Armstrong had a lasting career. He played from 1915 until his death in 1971. For more than 50 years, Armstrong toured the world and recorded jazz music. Like Bessie Smith's, Louis Armstrong's music is still an inspiration to people today.

Smith and Armstrong recorded together only three times in their career, but during these sessions they created nine hit records. Some of their best work included a popular song called "St. Louis Blues," and "You've Been a Good Old Wagon."

Backwater Blues

Bessie Smith paid close attention to the world around her. Many of her songs were about the troubles that African Americans dealt with. A song called "Backwater Blues" was one of her best-selling songs. This was a song she wrote herself.

"Backwater Blues" was about the flooding of the Ohio River. Smith had once seen the flooding with her own eyes. She saw the damage it caused and wrote about it. "Backwater Blues" was released when another flood occurred. This time it was the Mississippi River that flooded. Many believe the song was a huge success because of the flood.

Bessie Smith was a symbol of hope to many people. Her music helped them to be strong when times were hard. Unfortunately for Bessie, the good times would not last long. She found out that it was hard to stay at the top.

Because she had so many troubles, people sometimes said that Smith "lived the blues." She expressed her feelings about her hard times through her music.

Chapter 4:
A Style of Her Own

Bessie Smith is considered one of the most important blues singers in music history. She had a remarkable voice and a style of her own. Smith's natural talent truly made her a star.

People can learn about Bessie Smith's life by studying her songs. She lived "the blues" and her music was proof. Smith often sang about her troubles. Through her songs, Bessie Smith shared her life with the world.

Bessie Smith's music united people during a time when **segregation** divided people. People of all races and backgrounds experience love, heartache, and gloom. These are common feelings that all people can understand. Bessie Smith was popular because her music spoke to everyone.

African-American **oral tradition** and folk music inspired Bessie Smith. She was proud of her African-American heritage, or history and culture. Her music spoke about **discrimination** and the struggles that only African Americans could understand. Smith's **lyrics** were as important as her voice.

A Powerful Voice

Bessie Smith had power in her voice like no other blues singer of the time. Her voice was her instrument. Smith could use her voice to make sounds that amazed her audiences.

Smith's voice was rough. She often moaned and growled when she sang. At first, many people in the record industry felt her voice was too rough. They were used to the softer sound of the white pop singers. People later realized this was a part of the blues style.

Smith appeared fearless on stage. Her songs were as bold as she was. Smith was confident, and it could be heard in her voice. She could project her voice through an entire theater without a microphone. Smith never used a microphone until 1925, when she used one for the first time in the recording studio.

Smith had incredible control over her voice. While other blues singers often sounded as if they were shouting, Smith did not. This set her apart from the rest.

When Bessie Smith sang, as she is doing here, she usually did not use a microphone. Her voice was so loud and strong that she did not need one.

The Show Will Go On

After performing one evening in February 1925, Smith and several of her friends were invited to a party. The party was full of people eating, dancing, and having a good time. Smith and the other women went into the kitchen to have a snack.

They were minding their own business when a man came up and began to bully them. Smith did not like the way this man was acting toward her friends, so she slugged the man. Smith and the women went back to eating as though nothing had happened.

Later that evening, as they were leaving the party, the bully jumped out of the darkness and stabbed Bessie Smith with a knife. It is said that Smith chased after her attacker until she collapsed. An ambulance came and rushed her to the hospital.

Bessie Smith had a show to sing the next day. The doctors urged her to stay in the hospital, but she wanted the show to go on. She was released from the hospital later that morning. By two o'clock in the afternoon, Smith was back on stage. Bessie Smith would not let a bully stop the show.

Bessie Smith never let other people's ignorant opinions affect her pride in her heritage. No one could stop her from being passionate and successful.

Smith was a **passionate** woman. The audience could feel the emotion in her voice. It was Smith's **passion** that helped her to sing and to write music from the heart.

Life was hard for Bessie when her music stopped selling during the Great Depression. She no longer made a lot of money.

Chapter 5:
The Fall of Her Career

By the end of the 1920s, Bessie Smith's career had begun to fall. In 1929, many businesses began to close and the country went into the **Great Depression,** which lasted from 1929–1939. During these years, thousands of people lost their jobs and were living in **poverty.**

Many people could no longer afford to buy Smith's records. This was not good for Columbia. The company was losing money because fewer people were buying the records. Instead, people were seeing movies or listening to performances on the radio.

Bessie Smith was trying very hard to help boost her career. In 1929, she decided to star in a movie. Smith became one of the first African-American women to be on film. Smith performed in a short movie called *St. Louis Blues.* This is the only film ever made that shows Bessie Smith singing the blues.

In 1931, Smith recorded her last record for Columbia, called "Nobody Knows You When You're Down and Out." This record truly fit with Smith's life. Everyone wanted to be her friend when she was popular. However, when she was no longer rich and popular, people stopped being her friend.

Soon after, Columbia ended her recording contract. She had been working with Frank Walker and Columbia for more than eight years. Some believe that the Depression caused her career to fall. Others think that the problem she had with drinking was to blame.

By the early 1930s, businesses began to slowly open again. There were more jobs, and people were making money again. There was less **poverty,** and the country was doing well. This also brought about changes in the style of music. Blues music was no longer as popular. Jazz music had taken its place.

In the 1930s, Smith tried hard to make a comeback. Since the style of music had changed, she decided to sing songs other than the blues. This was often necessary for singers during this time. Because of this, Smith's singing crossed over into pop and jazz music.

Bessie continued to tour, but she was no longer making records with Columbia. Instead, she found other ways to bring her career back to life. She even tried to sing for a Broadway show, but had no luck.

John Hammond hired Bessie for the last record she would ever make.

In 1933, John Hammond hired Smith to record for the Okeh record company. Smith had known Hammond from the earlier days of her career. Smith recorded only one record for Okeh. It was the last record she ever made.

Bessie sings on stage during one of her shows. Her career was cut short by a terrible accident.

Chapter 6:
A Sad Ending

The recording session in 1933 helped Bessie Smith's career. She began performing in some larger theaters again. Then, on the morning of September 26, 1937, Bessie Smith and a friend, Richard Morgan, were driving along Route 61 near Clarksdale, Mississippi. Route 61 was a road that had two narrow lanes. It was also very dark with only a few lights. At about three o'clock in the morning, their car crashed into the back of a slow-moving truck that was at the side of the road. Smith's car flipped over when it hit the truck.

At the same time, a doctor named Hugh Smith (no relation to Bessie Smith) and a friend were driving down Route 61. Doctor Smith noticed the accident. When he got out of the car, he saw Bessie Smith lying in the middle of the road. He saw that Bessie's left arm had been nearly cut off. She was losing a lot of blood, which made it difficult for Doctor Smith to help her.

Doctor Smith pulled Bessie onto the side of the highway. The entire right side of her body was crushed, and she was having trouble breathing. Doctor Smith quickly sent his friend to a nearby house to call for an ambulance.

Time was running out for Bessie Smith. She continued to lose blood. While waiting for the ambulance to arrive, another car crashed into Doctor Smith's car. The car was traveling at high speeds. It had nearly hit the people standing on the side of the road.

Two people in the other car had also been injured. Doctor Smith now had three people to save. The ambulance and police arrived shortly after the second crash. They took Bessie Smith and Morgan to a hospital in Clarksdale.

Richard Morgan survived the crash. Sadly, Bessie Smith had lost too much blood and died later that evening.

Remembering Bessie Smith

On October 4, 1937, a funeral was held in Philadelphia for Bessie Smith. Thousands of people came to pay their respect for Smith. Philadelphia had never seen so many people come to honor an African American. At that moment, the world recognized the importance of Bessie Smith's life.

Bessie holds a feathered hat from one of her costumes. Today, many performers wear elaborate costumes like Bessie did.

Bessie Smith was brave and strong-willed, and worked hard to earn equal treatment for African Americans. To many, Smith was a hero. She lived at a time when racism, **discrimination,** and **segregation** were everywhere. However, Smith proved to herself and the entire world that African Americans had the power to succeed. She was proud to be an African American.

Many people remember Bessie Smith today. Her musical style and talent have inspired many musicians. Smith's music has shaped other singers, like rock-and-roll star Janis Joplin and rhythm-and-blues star Aretha Franklin.

Bessie Smith's grave was unmarked for nearly 37 years. At the time of her death, no one would spend the money to buy her a gravestone. In 1970, Janis Joplin and others bought a gravestone for Smith. Joplin had the following words carved into the stone:

The Greatest Blues Singer
in the World Will Never Stop Singing
Bessie Smith
1895–1937

Bessie Smith had many great accomplishments in her lifetime, but she did not receive any awards until after her death. In 1980, she was inducted into the Blues Hall of Fame. Nine years later, she was inducted into the Rock and Roll Hall of Fame.

Janis Joplin was a big fan of Bessie's and even helped buy Bessie a gravestone.

Aretha Franklin is accepting an award for her singing in this photo. She learned a lot about singing and style by listening to the music of Bessie Smith.

Bessie Smith was more than just a great blues singer. She was a voice of courage and determination for all who have ever suffered. She was, and still is, an inspiration to people of all races.

Aretha Franklin

Aretha Franklin is one of the most popular rhythm-and-blues singers today. Many call her the "Queen of Soul." Like Bessie Smith, Franklin was born in Tennessee. Her father was a Baptist preacher. Franklin spent many Sundays in church with her father. Church music, which is also called gospel music, was Franklin's first musical influence.

Franklin began singing gospel, or church music, at an early age. Her style is a mixture of gospel and blues music. This mixture is called the rhythm and blues, or soul music.

Like Bessie Smith, Aretha Franklin is recognized for her powerful voice. Her **lyrics** have inspired many people, especially women. One of her most famous songs is called "Respect." It talks about treating women in a fair way.

Aretha Franklin has won several Grammy Awards and a Lifetime Achievement Award in 1995. Aretha Franklin was inducted into the Rock and Roll Hall of Fame in 1987.

Glossary

audition   process an actor or musician goes through to be hired

classic blues   blues that were sung by women. Bessie Smith was a classic blues singer.

country blues   blues that were sung by men. Country blues came from the songs that slaves would sing.

discriminate   an act of discrimination (see below)

discrimination   prejudice or unjust behavior to others based on differences in age, color or gender

Great Depression   the years from 1929 to 1939, when millions of Americans were jobless and homeless

Harlem Renaissance   period of time in the 1920s and 1930s when many African Americans went to Harlem, a neighborhood in New York City. Many African American writers, musicians, and artists who lived there became well known during this time.

headliner   starring act of a show

jazz   American music started by African Americans in the early 1900s. Its main characteristics are a three line pattern, a clear beat, and improvisation.

lyrics   words of a song

minstrel show   traveling show with African Americans who performed a musical story. Minstrel shows often had singers, dancers, actors, comedians, and jugglers.

oral tradition   custom, idea, or belief that is handed down by speaking

passion   very strong feeling, such as love or anger

passionate   having feelings of passion

poverty   state of being extremely poor

segregate   keep separate. Laws in the United States often segregated African Americans from white people.

segregation   act of segregating

vaudeville   stage show that had between eight and fourteen separate acts, including singing, dancing, magicians, jugglers, and comedy acts

Timeline

1894- Smith is born April 15th, in Chattanooga, Tennessee.

1912- Smith gets her first job in The Moses Stokes minstrel show.

Smith meets Gertrude "Ma" Rainey.

1913- Smith moves to Atlanta, Georgia.

Smith starts touring the South.

1918- The first advertisement for Smith is published in a Maryland newspaper.

1920- Smith moves to Philadelphia, Pennsylvania.

Mamie Smith (no relation) records the first blues song.

1923- Smith makes an agreement with Columbia to record her music.

Smith records her first song, called "Down Hearted Blues."

Smith marries Jack Gee.

1925- Smith records music with Louis Armstrong.

Smith uses a microphone for the first time to record "Cake Walking Babies."

1929- Smith appears in her first movie, called *St. Louis Blues.*

1931- Columbia ends Smith's record contract.

1933- Smith records the last song of her career for Okeh records.

1936- Smith sings at the Apollo Theater in New York.

1937- Smith dies in a car accident on September 26th in Mississippi.

1970- Janis Joplin and others purchase a gravestone for Smith.

1980- Smith is inducted into the Blues Hall of Fame.

1989- Smith is inducted into the Rock and Roll Hall of Fame.

Further Information

Further reading

Davis, Francis. *The History of the Blues: The Roots, the Music, the People—From Charlie Patton to Robert Cray.* New York: Hyperion Press, 1995.

Gaines, Ann. *The Harlem Renaissance in American History.* Berkeley Heights, N.J.: Enslow Publishers, 2002.

Thomas, Roger. *Jazz and Blues.* Chicago: Heinemann Library, 1998.

Addresses

Chattanooga African-American Museum
     200 East Martin Luther King
     Chattanooga, TN 37403

MENC: The National Association for Music Education
     1806 Robert Fulton Drive
     Reston, VA 20191

National Association for the
     Advancement of Colored
     People (NAACP)
     4805 Mt. Hope Drive
     Baltimore, MD 21215

Smithsonian Anacostia Museum & Center for African-American Culture
     1901 Fort Place, SE
     Washington, DC 20020

Index